QUOTES TO INSPIRE & ELUCIDATE

DAVID M. SOMERFLECK

"

Over a Month's Worth of Inspiring & Educational Quotes on Digital Marketing and Business to Help You Transform How You Work and Live

by David M. Somerfleck
https://boldly.blue

Professionals have *processes and then procedures* they use that empower them to work easily and efficiently.

These processes and procedures help them ensure *their clients* achieve the results they want and need.

Don't be afraid to *expect* professionals to have processes and procedures in place for how they work with you...even if they're in a lesser known field such as digital marketing.

 BOLDLY.BLUE

 BUSINESSGROWTH

....the reality is that most people (aka the public at large or wantrepreneurs with no skin in the game) see "Shark Tank" and think that all they need to be multi-millionaires overnight is to come up with a cool idea and pitch it to a group of fatcats. You can't have sales without business development and you can't have business development without sales. It's like digital marketing without SEO, eCommerce, branding, design, and content. It's popular and easy to see complex processes as simple one and done single items, but it's not the real world.

When we break down goals into realistic point by point objectives needed to achieve that goal, then break down steps in a chain needed to attain each objective point, then figure out how we have to behave and who we have to become to put that chain into action, things get done quickly.

FOLLOW- UP

Some of the most common processes we use in business range from screening our ideal customers or clients to ensure that they're a good fit for our business and /or services and then, after that, onboard them, where we train them in how we work, why some processes must be followed a certain way, and then impliment a follow-up process to maintain communication.

Find online tools to help you automate each step in your own process to make life - and business - easier and more efficient.

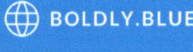 BOLDLY.BLUE

 BUSINESSGROWTH

❝

A marketing consultant I knew was hired by a family-owned agency because he was dating one of the family members. Clients were leaving the agency in droves and this person didn't understand his duties or how to execute them.

The agency owner's solution was to encourage the consultant to spend more time with senior staff who were more experienced; hoping this exposure would give the consultant insight and dedication. This consultant did not change or grow so the agency owner asked several of us for input. I told the agency owner that until this employee was shown direct benefits and need to improve there was no motivation for him to do so.

Until there is a perceived need for growth, there isn't likely to be actual growth.

 BOLDLY.BLUE

 BUSINESSGROWTH

FOLLOW- UP

The old adage "you can lead a horse to water, but you can't make it drink," is as true todoay as it was when it first originated. Your employees (and friends or family members for that matter) have to see (and often feel) a reason to take specific measured actions before they will do so. Dr. Elizabeth Kubler-Ross documented this in her work on dealing with the loss of a loved one, where people often negotiated or denied rather than deal with what was in front of their faces. This is just as relevant in business as it is in relationships.

BOLDLY.BLUE   BUSINESSGROWTH

According to leading industry sources, 82% of smartphone shoppers conducted "near me" searches.

This means that sophisticated consumers want to find local businesses. Local SEO helps businesses accomplish that. If we add eCommerce to that business' online presence, we're more likely to increase sales even further since we make it easier for consumers to make purchases.

Local SEO and eCommerce when used properly, and in tandem, can be powerful for the organized and committed business owner.

 BOLDLY.BLUE

 BUSINESSGROWTH

FOLLOW- UP

When I was a certified small business and startup mentor for several Non-Profit Organizations (NPOs), after several months I came to realize that most business owners saw websites as "one and done" items rather than as company portals through which valuable and important processes could go through -while concurrently promoting their business online 24/7 through multiple online channels. Set your goals higher and ask yourself "how can we automate what takes up so much of our time and energy" and "how can we learn from and mirror the strategies of larger, more profitable competitors?"

 BOLDLY.BLUE    BUSINESSGROWTH

"

According to eCommerce research studies 88% of consumers perform research before buying products online.

For the entrepreneur this means it helps your sales if you have detailed product descriptions, photos of your items from different viewpoints, details about product use, reviews wherever possible, and more information - as if you yourself were the shopper.

When you look at your business from the perspective of the consumer, you can notice things you might not have before.

 BOLDLY.BLUE

 BUSINESSGROWTH

FOLLOW- UP

If you expect your customers or clients to be selective, you have good reason. There are plenty of global powerhouse companies competing with yours. Go where they can't. Do what they can't. Offer what they don't know to do or can't. Build trust, showcase your personal care and experience. Every day I see business websites with no background on staff or owners or services provided, that don't let me pay or schedule or that have little to no content, with ads for "get your free website" on the bottom of every page. Do all you can to stand out, show care and professionalism, and make it easy for your ideal customer to work with you.

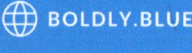 BOLDLY.BLUE    BUSINESSGROWTH

❝

According to multiple leading industry sources consumers are 71% more likely to purchase based on social media referrals.

What this means for the business owner or entrepreneur is that it pays to advertise your services or products on social media. Doing so increases exposure, brand awareness, and over time, familiarity and sense of the purchase being "referred" to them by a trusted source.

When you expand reach, you expand returns.

 **BOLDLY.BLUE**

 **BUSINESSGROWTH**

FOLLOW-UP

ou can successfully and smartly advertise your goods or services on social media 24/7 through automated and scheduled paid advertising (also called PPC for "Pay Per Click"). Such advertising should be special limited time offers, discounts, "buy one get one free" offers, bundle package offers, free downloads in exchange for a subscription to your blog (so you can build your marketing list), upcoming free and paid events. At no point should there be personal commentary, as that's more appropriate for personal social media accounts.   By promoting thoughtful and needed content you can reach more consumers more often, who can in-turn show their friends, family, or other staff members.

 BOLDLY.BLUE    BUSINESSGROWTH

Gardens grow when they're watered regularly, given proper soil, proper sunlight, roots are given room to expand, weeds are removed, and the plants are kept apart from dangerous threats.

Digital marketing, can 'grow your garden' when it's equally maintained. Think of the website as the plant, then content marketing are branches, **SEO** are roots and trunk, flowers are special offers, viruses and malware as weeds, seeds are paid ads and videos, content repurposing in the form of podcasts or videos or guest blogging are seeds carried on the wind. Seasons are competitors and changing economic conditions.

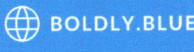 BOLDLY.BLUE

 BUSINESSGROWTH

FOLLOW- UP

In the old days when the internet was still new, websites were called "portals" through which all related activities were done and needs met. We would download payroll, timesheets, meetings minutes, training materials, schedule meetings, pay bills, pay for rentals or services, buy goods, buy tickets to events or talks, order food, and check status updates. Look at the company website as a 24 hour marketing machine for your business that can serve multiple purposes at the same time, and from multiple perspectives. Just as the website needs updating, back-ups, security; it can provide customers everything they'd need or want.

 BOLDLY.BLUE

 BUSINESSGROWTH

> There was a business owner years ago who was angry that their *supposedly* free DIY website had not made them number one in Google or helped their business expand into new markets.
>
> When I asked them why they believed that such *could* be the case, their response was that many people online (none of whom they knew personally or professionally) had told them it could be that way.
>
> They had never bothered to verify or conduct any due diligence of their own, or ask any experts, so ended up losing tens of thousands of dollars in lost revenue before finally taking corrective action.

You get out what you put in.

 **BOLDLY.BLUE**    **BUSINESSGROWTH**

FOLLOW-UP

When we expect something that cost us nothing, that we expended little to no effort on, to attract valuable customers for our business, we're kidding ourselves with idealized thinking. Lesson in point: Decades ago I attended a job interview for a "dream job" and intended to show my "free" DIY website to the interviewer to showcase my work portfolio and testimonials. When I opened the laptop to show them the website, it had been deleted by the "free" hosting company. I was never told why and legally they didn't *need* a reason. I immediately paid for hosting, a premium account, created my own website, posted my content again, and never had that problem again. The website was "free" but cost me that one job. Why risk your business' appearance and future when you don't need to? If you aren't committed to growing a business sufficiently to invest in it modestly and logically, than it's an idea or hobby you still have lingering uncertainties about. Be honest.

BOLDLY.BLUE #BUSINESSGROWTH

Many business owners refuse to invest in marketing or advertising that could empower them to grow, seeing it as something they'll get to later.

Then they wonder later why nobody is calling them and sales stay flat or plummet.

In life, and especially in business, we get out what we are willing to put in. It's the law of cause and effect. For every action there is an equal or greater reaction.

The person who has no time to study doesn't learn that subject. The business owner who sees no benefit from investing in marketing and advertising doesn't increase growth through those means.

 BOLDLY.BLUE

 BUSINESSGROWTH

FOLLOW-UP

When the question is one of commitment and dedication, you find that many businesses that are new so often fall to the wayside because the owner(s) are not fully committed. They don't want to invest financially or time-wise or energetically in something they themselves are not sure of yet. As a mentor, I found this to be the primary reason businesses would fail, within their first 2-3 years if not sooner. I could lay the path out for them, offer to guide them, tell them directly what to do and why, and even offer to be available to provide more information as needed, and pride or hubris or fear of success (or failure) would prevent them from proceeding. However, those small few that went on to garner huge profit margins were 100% dedicated toward a larger vision of themselves and their business. Failure was not an option. Not appearing professional or above-board was not an option. Not being their very best in every way was not an option. Putting in the hours, the investment capital, was a given.

🌐 BOLDLY.BLUE   #️⃣ BUSINESSGROWTH

Freelancers struggling to find high-paying clients and rewarding work face multiple issues they have to resolve in order to move forward. The primary one is who they are engaging with as an ideal fit. The secondary issue is communication once that client is identified and engaged.

We have to be The Expert In The Room at all times or we risk our best efforts being commoditized and underutilized. Screen for proper fit, onboard for setting efficient processes and workflow, and seek out repeatable ways to cultivate interest on behalf of those with actual need .

 BOLDLY.BLUE

 BUSINESSGROWTH

FOLLOW- UP

You may not be able to be the "Alpha and the Omega" but you can (and should) be the one-stop resource for your ideal customers or clients. Just because you may be a "solopreneur" single individual freelance worker doesn't mean you can't have the same systems and processes in place that a large marketing agency employs or that a large business uses. A restaurant has a "Point Of Sale" (POS) system to charge diners. You can and should have eCommerce to take payments across multiple platforms.

 BOLDLY.BLUE    BUSINESSGROWTH

> You can't build and grow a successful business by yourself, for yourself.
>
> DIY can only get you so far before it ceases to return dividends. We all need help at some point.
>
> In digital marketing there are plenty of DIY approaches. But would you bet the future of your business on a generic, automated template builder? If achieving specific goals matters to you, you'll be more likely to hire a professional.
>
> *When entrepreneurs ask me when DIY marketing is appropriate, I say it is when achieving specific goals don't matter.*

 BOLDLY.BLUE

 BUSINESSGROWTH

❝

From a marketing perspective, I think there are 5 key components used in business today, which are important to overview in-depth. They would be intent, proper building out of long-term and short-term goals, the concept of repurposing, perspective of communication, and making sure a comprehensive marketing as well as its execution are written out. The digital marketing plan comes with robust SWOT analysis, SMART goals, ideal consumer/avatar analysis as well as Unique Selling Proposition (USP). By breaking these components down into incremental steps in respective order, they become more manageable and easier to create the path of marketing strategy to build relationships with clientele."

 BOLDLY.BLUE

 BUSINESSGROWTH

> There's an ancient Arabian legend that tells of a stranger who put loaves of spiced bread out across the northern border of town. The villagers, hungry for food, were delighted by their bounty and sang the stranger's praises. While the villagers rejoiced, the stranger easily plundered the southern section of town.

Focus in growing a business is so important if you expect to reach self-sufficiency and economic independence. Be wary of "free" DIY solutions that promise the moon and stars for nothing, wanting immediate gratification, or uninformed random opinions of the inexperienced, rather put in the work, focus on structure and processes needed to build a foundation instead.

 BOLDLY.BLUE

 BUSINESSGROWTH

As business owners interested in growing a company and possibly a brand, we find success through failure.

Usually, aspiring entrepreneurs reading blog posts encouraging them to "just jump in!" and that "anyone can do it, all you have to do is try!" will follow the siren call. Experienced business owners know the path ahead is fraught with potholes, wild-eyed hitchhikers, broken signs, incomplete maps, and unmarked roads.

It's through failing, acknowledging failures, and <u>deciding</u> to learn from them, that we ensure costly mistakes don't reoccur. This cements the road ahead, writes the map, posts the signs.

 **BOLDLY.BLUE**    **BUSINESSGROWTH**

> There are different tools to accomplish different tasks and different types of plans in order to achieve different type of goals. There are different types of processes that help us use tools, fulfill plans and even to define specific goals we wish to achieve.
>
> You wouldn't go to a dentist for your SEO, a mechanic for your marketing plan, or an anonymous generic DIY tool you have virtually no experience using to promote the future of your business.
>
> **The right tool to fit the right task**, the right process to achieve the appropriate goal, and informed planning to get us from Point A to Point B. Those approaches are more likely to work every time.

 BOLDLY.BLUE

 BUSINESSGROWTH

"

When we look at startups and nonprofits and small business ventures, whatever form business takes, the odds of success are statistically very low.

Most businesses will be a memory within five years of starting if not sooner.

This is why brutal self-honesty is so important. Own your failures. Be proud of the efforts taken, even if they resulted in loss, but only if you learned from them. What oversights were there, what role did pride play, what role overwhelm, ego, inexperience?

We can learn as much from failure, if not more, than we can from success.

 BOLDLY.BLUE   BUSINESSGROWTH

When startup founders and small business owners ask me *why their business is not succeeding*, the answers are always crystal clear after talking with them for a few minutes.

The solution however can be like taking a team hiking up a mountain that is covered with thick, heavy mud.

Often times we seek to climb a mountain with no map, no tools, and no team. Other times we seek to climb the wrong mountain that has no trail and no gold.

Sometimes we have to look at the tools, the map, the team, or the mountain.

 BOLDLY.BLUE

 BUSINESSGROWTH

> **At the end of our lives** we don't wish we had more things or have hurt more people. We wish we could have loved more people more honestly, left more behind, lived more, and lived more *freely*.
>
> Rather than spend our time and energy debating obvious truths with others or checking a social media feed to see if someone approves, ***create art*** that gives voice to your innermost being, build a business that makes the world a better place, love more without fear.

 BOLDLY.BLUE

 BUSINESSGROWTH

> When you look at *social media* ask yourself if what you read is truth that can help you in your life and business, information you didn't know before...or if it is just another infomercial....marketing content that is selling another "get-rich-quick" scheme sold by yet another magical guru guy.
>
> *What you digest should either help you or it is ego-driven pabulum you most likely don't need.*

 **BOLDLY.BLUE**    **SOCIALMEDIA**

"

A 'revelation' is when we see things as they are, not how we wish they were. I consulted a business owner once with $500,000 of debt and bleeding money. When I suggested changes that experience told me could transform the business, the owner resisted. When I pointed out that it was fear of the unknown coupled with a need to feel in control, and not logical reason, and that they had nothing to lose and everything to gain, the owner relented and began to cooperate. The changes could then bring improvements.

Internal work is often more valuable than external.

 BOLDLY.BLUE    BUSINESSGROWTH

"

Many businesses buckled under COVID's unpredictable weight through no fault of their own. And yet how many businesses could've been better prepared? Restaurants and others that could've offered home delivery, online ordering, local SEO, online marketing to grow locally but were not? Business management is more than just running around putting out fires. It's also planning for such crises.

If you're doing everything you reasonably can, and expect the unexpected through examining your business Strengths, Weakness, Opportunities, and potential Threats you may not be prepared for every eventuality but you'll have fewer.

 BOLDLY.BLUE

 BUSINESSGROWTH

> People on *social media* who post cruel or unhelpful comments are doing so, whether they know it or not, from a need to satisfy their ego. Their goal is to wound you with their words. That is no more helpful to you, or your business, than stepping on a nail.
>
> Kick the nail away or pick it up and put it in the trash, where it belongs. *See the difference between the valuable and the worthless and you'll save countless years of strife and get more done in less time.*

 BOLDLY.BLUE   SOCIALMEDIA

"

Social media can attract scavengers and shape-shifters by its very nature: What networking group can you go to where attendees can hide their faces and use others' names while mocking attendees or providing hateful critiques of sincere efforts to improve your life or help others? Instead what if we looked for information we could verify? What if we asked how this view informs us, lifts us up, or ultimately if it is yet another bot, bored teen, lonely soul, phishing scam, or ego-driven put down?

BOLDLY.BLUE   SOCIALMEDIA

❝

Your *'Unique Selling Proposition*" is a marketing term that means finding what defines your offerings in business and approach. It's that so-called 'sweet spot' where your services, products, experience all intersect with what your local and possibly national markets need, want, understand, and value. When you find your USP you'll know it because writing out mission statements, explaining your value, detailing the benefits of what you do to investors or prospective clients, all will be as effortless as sipping tea.

 BOLDLY.BLUE

 MARKETING

❝

Your "*Unique Selling Proposition*" or USP, is finding points where several factors unite: You excel at doing it, you love doing it, you would do it regardless of economic circumstances, local or national competitors can't do it the way you do, how you do it and the services or products appeal to an undeserved need and possibly group, it fulfills emotional and practical needs, doing it does not violate ethical, legal or moral principals, and of course you can get paid to do it.

 BOLDLY.BLUE

 MARKETING

"

Feeling stuck in business or in life is common. There's no shame in it at all. It often comes from childhood memories of feeling trapped within restrictive situations or environments.

Saying 'yes" to your dreams means asking if we toil under the yoke of unstated laws, what those may be, and then deciding to disobey them.

The great writer Samuel Johnson said 'Fear is implanted in us as a preservative from evil; but its duty, like that of other passions, is not to overbear reason, but to assist it; nor should it be suffered to tyrannize in the imagination, to raise phantoms of horror, or beset life with supernumerary distresses.'

In other words, once we understand *why* something is not working we can go about deciding whether or not we really still need it.

 BOLDLY.BLUE   MINDSET

"

When business owners talk about wanting to be *#1 in Google*, it's vital they understand that Google is a giant search program that presents its findings to potential consumers and clients, not a magical wizard who can be bribed or tricked. In order to be listed on that first page, let alone in that first *place*, you would need to know your market well, local and national competitors, and have ways to compete with them across multiple platforms over time.

Competitors aren't going anywhere, can change and evolve over time, and so you need a way to cut through the clatter if you're going to be found and then heard.

 BOLDLY.BLUE

 DIGITALMARKETING

ROI, or Return On Investment, is the difference between spending money without knowing what it is going toward, or withholding investing due to apathy or confusion, and investing money in order to achieve important and measurable outcomes.

Experienced business owners who have been through tough times and made it know what they're investing for and why it matters.

They would gladly invest $3,000 if they felt it would earn them $30,000 months later.

 BOLDLY.BLUE   **BUSINESSGROWTH**

> When a business owner asks *'how much is a website?'* or *'how much is SEO?'* it implies that they are purchasing items, not investing in processes to build a business.
>
> The way we as professionals can help mediate this view is to identify costly problems they need solved, goals they want achieved, then ask what value there would be in solving those problems, achieving those goals.
>
> Then we can explain that we can use digital marketing to solve those problems and reach those goals if they are committed to growth and toward investing to move forward. Then if they are committed we can discuss budget estimates and ranges. **But a tool by itself can't solve a problem that isn't yet identified...just as a hammer can't build a house.**

 BOLDLY.BLUE

 DIGITALMARKETING

❝

Your *Customer Acquisition Cost*, or CAC, tells you what you should invest in order to achieve the most important results in the least amount of time with the least strenuous expense of energy as well.

It is knowing what you spent on marketing and advertising in one month, quarter, or year, and then dividing that number by how many customers you attracted for that period of time, then deciding if that approach is working for your business or not.

BOLDLY.BLUE   # CUSTOMERACQUISITION

"

As a Digital Marketing expert I tell struggling business owners that *a website in and of itself won't help them*. Filling in a generic DIY template is like buying a stack of business cards. Without interested recipients they are empty gestures.

Instead, business owners need deliberately organized structure, clearly defined markets to sell to, means and ways to market, and high-value problems to solve. Once those are identified, a website can use SEO to be found, eCommerce to take payments, content to attract and nurture lead generation, repurposing to expand reach, design to cultivate patronage and ultimately then use a website to channel all those components *through*.

BOLDLY.BLUE

DIGITALMARKETING

> There was a museum with no guards whose priceless artwork was vandalized and stolen. When museum administrators hired and then trained guards the vandals and thieves could no longer gain access.
>
> Your mind and energy are like that artwork.
>
> When you *guard your time*, your creativity, your passions, and exercise discipline, forces that detract you from pursuing your passion no longer gain access to lead you astray. *Guard your time and what you do with your time as you would priceless art* - because in a way, it is.

BOLDLY.BLUE   PRODUCTIVITY

Critics can attack you for being authentic <u>or</u> inauthentic. They may not approve of how you dress, how you talk, what you look like, or the content you produce.

It's for that reason that you may as well be yourself, to your *utmost*, as truly and as accurately as you can.

That way, if you fail at something at least you were honest with yourself and you did your best. And if you succeed at something you know it was achieved your way. Ultimately, progressing gradually and sincerely in life, and in business, is what counts most. *Apathy and negativity are easier to manifest and therefore more common.*

 BOLDLY.BLUE

 AUTHENTICITY

"

Growing a sustainable and profitable business is a group effort we have to either lead as The Expert or collaborate within.

If problems in growth persist, there are deficits within that dynamic, not necessarily with SEO or content marketing or a company website.

Those aspects of digital marketing must work as *part* of a larger organized plan to be effective over time.

If there is no competent, informed, objective leadership or no true open collaboration, all the SEO in the world is irrelevant.

 BOLDLY.BLUE   BUSINESSGROWTH

>

Hustle culture is the philosophy of working harder, not smarter, of the immediate over the earned and established and lasting.

Actions taken that are not based on deliberately researched information and then guided by informed, objective decisions will ultimately exhaust and bankrupt.

Beware the overly simplistic.

BOLDLY.BLUE   PRODUCTIVITY

WWW.BOLDLY.BLUE

"

Want Even More?

Read other works by David M. Somerfleck for valuable insights.

-

David M. Somerfleck, www.boldly.blue

TODAY'S
QUOTE

www.ingramcontent.com/pod-product-compliance
Lightning Source LLC
Chambersburg PA
CBHW040248220526
45473CB00001B/410